HAL•LEONARD®
VIOLIN
PLAY-ALONG

AUDIO
ACCESS
INCLUDED

POP covers

M000103529

PLAYBACK+
Speed • Pitch • Balance • Loop

To access audio visit:
www.halleonard.com/mylibrary

Enter Code
3378-9985-6009-5048

ISBN 978-1-4950-7375-5

Jon Vriesacker, violin
Audio arrangements by Peter Deneff
Recorded and Produced by Jake Johnson
at Paradyme Productions

HAL•LEONARD®
7777 W. BLUEMOUND RD. P.O.BOX 13819 MILWAUKEE, WI 53213

Visit Hal Leonard Online at
www.halleonard.com

HAL•LEONARD®
VIOLIN PLAY-ALONG

AUDIO ACCESS INCLUDED

POP COVERS

CONTENTS

Brave

Words and Music by Sara Bareilles and Jack Antonoff

Call Me Maybe

Words and Music by Carly Rae Jepsen, Joshua Ramsay and Tavish Crowe

Thinking Out Loud

Words and Music by Ed Sheeran and Amy Wadge

9

Hey, Soul Sister

Words and Music by Pat Monahan, Espen Lind and Amund Bjorklund

Jar of Hearts

Words and Music by Barrett Yeretsian, Christina Perri and Drew Lawrence

Roar

Words and Music by Katy Perry, Lukasz Gottwald, Max Martin, Bonnie McKee and Henry Walter

Rolling in the Deep

Words and Music by Adele Adkins and Paul Epworth

Stay with Me

Words and Music by Sam Smith, James Napier, William Edward Phillips, Tom Petty and Jeff Lynne

HAL•LEONARD®
VIOLIN
PLAY-ALONG

AUDIO
ACCESS
INCLUDED

The Violin Play-Along Series
Play your favorite songs quickly and easily!

Just follow the music, listen to the CD or online audio to hear how the violin should sound, and then play along using the separate backing tracks. The audio files are enhanced so you can adjust the recordings to any tempo without changing pitch!

1. Bluegrass
00842152 Book/Online Audio ..$14.99

2. Popular Songs
00842153 Book/CD Pack $14.99

3. Classical
00842154 Book/Online Audio ..$14.99

4. Celtic
00842155 Book/Online Audio ..$14.99

5. Christmas Carols
00842156 Book/Online Audio ..$14.99

6. Holiday Hits
00842157 Book/CD Pack $14.99

7. Jazz
00842196 Book/CD Pack $14.99

8. Country Classics
00842230 Book/Online Audio ..$12.99

9. Country Hits
00842231 Book/CD Pack $14.99

10. Bluegrass Favorites
00842232 Book/CD Pack $14.99

11. Bluegrass Classics
00842233 Book/CD Pack $14.99

12. Wedding Classics
00842324 Book/Online Audio ..$14.99

13. Wedding Favorites
00842325 Book/CD Pack $14.99

14. Blues Classics
00842427 Book/CD Pack $14.99

15. Stephane Grappelli
00842428 Book/Online Audio ...$14.99

16. Folk Songs
00842429 Book/CD Pack $14.99

17. Christmas Favorites
00842478 Book/CD Pack $14.99

18. Fiddle Hymns
00842499 Book/Online Audio ...$14.99

19. Lennon & McCartney
00842564 Book/CD Pack $14.99

20. Irish Tunes
00842565 Book/Online Audio ...$14.99

21. Andrew Lloyd Webber
00842566 Book/Online Audio ...$14.99

22. Broadway Hits
00842567 Book/CD Pack $14.99

23. Pirates of the Caribbean
00842625 Book/Online Audio ...$14.99

24. Rock Classics
00842640 Book/CD Pack $14.99

25. Classical Masterpieces
00842642 Book/CD Pack $14.99

26. Elementary Classics
00842643 Book/CD Pack $14.99

27. Classical Favorites
00842646 Book/CD Pack $14.99

28. Classical Treasures
00842647 Book/CD Pack $14.99

29. Disney Favorites
00842648 Book/CD Pack $14.99

30. Disney Hits
00842649 Book/CD Pack $14.99

31. Movie Themes
00842706 Book/CD Pack $14.99

32. Favorite Christmas Songs
00102110 Book/CD Pack $14.99

33. Hoedown
00102161 Book/CD Pack $14.99

34. Barn Dance
00102568 Book/CD Pack $14.99

35. Lindsey Stirling
00109715 Book/Online Audio ...$19.99

36. Hot Jazz
00110373 Book/CD Pack $14.99

37. Taylor Swift
00116361 Book/CD Pack $14.99

38. John Williams
00116367 Book/CD Pack $14.99

39. Italian Songs
00116368 Book/CD Pack $14.99

41. Johann Strauss
00121041 Book/CD Pack $14.99

42. Light Classics
00121935 Book/Online Audio ...$14.99

43. Light Orchestra Pop
00122126 Book/Online Audio ...$14.99

44. French Songs
00122123 Book/Online Audio ...$14.99

45. Lindsey Stirling Hits
00123128 Book/Online Audio ...$19.99

46. Piazzolla Tangos
48022997 Book/Online Audio ...$16.99

47. Light Masterworks
00124149 Book/Online Audio ...$14.99

48. Frozen
00126478 Book/Online Audio ...$14.99

49. Pop/Rock
00130216 Book/Online Audio ...$14.99

50. Songs for Beginners
00131417 Book/Online Audio ...$14.99

51. Chart Hits for Beginners
00131418 Book/Online Audio ...$14.99

52. Celtic Rock
00148756 Book/Online Audio ...$14.99

53. Rockin' Classics
00148768 Book/Online Audio ...$14.99

54. Scottish Folksongs
00148779 Book/Online Audio ...$14.99

55. Wicked
00148780 Book/Online Audio ...$14.99

56. The Sound of Music
00148782 Book/Online Audio ...$14.99

57. Movie Music
00150962 Book/Online Audio ...$14.99

58. The Piano Guys – Wonders
00151837 Book/Online Audio ...$19.99

59. Worship Favorites
00152534 Book/Online Audio ...$14.99

60. The Beatles
00155293 Book/Online Audio ...$14.99

61. Star Wars: The Force Awakens
00157648 Book/Online Audio ...$14.99

62. Star Wars
00157650 Book/Online Audio ...$14.99

7777 W. BLUEMOUND RD. P.O. BOX 13819 MILWAUKEE, WI 53213

www.halleonard.com

0916

HAL·LEONARD INSTRUMENTAL PLAY-ALONG

Your favorite songs are arranged just for solo instrumentalists with this outstanding series. Each book includes a great full-accompaniment play-along audio so you can sound just like a pro! Check out **www.halleonard.com** to see all the titles available.

Chart Hits
All About That Bass • All of Me • Happy • Radioactive • Roar • Say Something • Shake It Off • A Sky Full of Stars • Someone like Me • Stay with Me • Thinking Out Loud • Uptown Funk.

____	00146207	Flute	$12.99
____	00146208	Clarinet	$12.99
____	00146209	Alto Sax	$12.99
____	00146210	Tenor Sax	$12.99
____	00146211	Trumpet	$12.99
____	00146212	Horn	$12.99
____	00146213	Trombone	$12.99
____	00146214	Violin	$12.99
____	00146215	Viola	$12.99
____	00146216	Cello	$12.99

Coldplay
Clocks • Every Teardrop Is a Waterfall • Fix You • In My Place • Lost! • Paradise • The Scientist • Speed of Sound • Trouble • Violet Hill • Viva La Vida • Yellow.

____	00103337	Flute	$12.99
____	00103338	Clarinet	$12.99
____	00103339	Alto Sax	$12.99
____	00103340	Tenor Sax	$12.99
____	00103341	Trumpet	$12.99
____	00103342	Horn	$12.99
____	00103343	Trombone	$12.99
____	00103344	Violin	$12.99
____	00103345	Viola	$12.99
____	00103346	Cello	$12.99

Disney Greats
Arabian Nights • Hawaiian Roller Coaster Ride • It's a Small World • Look Through My Eyes • Yo Ho (A Pirate's Life for Me) • and more.

____	00841934	Flute	$12.99
____	00841935	Clarinet	$12.99
____	00841936	Alto Sax	$12.99
____	00841937	Tenor Sax	$12.95
____	00841938	Trumpet	$12.99
____	00841939	Horn	$12.95
____	00841940	Trombone	$12.95
____	00841941	Violin	$12.99
____	00841942	Viola	$12.95
____	00841943	Cello	$12.99
____	00842078	Oboe	$12.99

Great Themes
Bella's Lullaby • Chariots of Fire • Get Smart • Hawaii Five-O Theme • I Love Lucy • The Odd Couple • Spanish Flea • and more.

____	00842468	Flute	$12.99
____	00842469	Clarinet	$12.99
____	00842470	Alto Sax	$12.99
____	00842471	Tenor Sax	$12.99
____	00842472	Trumpet	$12.99
____	00842473	Horn	$12.99
____	00842474	Trombone	$12.99
____	00842475	Violin	$12.99
____	00842476	Viola	$12.99
____	00842477	Cello	$12.99

Lennon & McCartney Favorites
All You Need Is Love • A Hard Day's Night • Here, There and Everywhere • Hey Jude • Let It Be • Nowhere Man • Penny Lane • She Loves You • When I'm Sixty-Four • and more.

____	00842600	Flute	$12.99
____	00842601	Clarinet	$12.99
____	00842602	Alto Sax	$12.99
____	00842603	Tenor Sax	$12.99
____	00842604	Trumpet	$12.99
____	00842605	Horn	$12.99
____	00842607	Violin	$12.99
____	00842608	Viola	$12.99
____	00842609	Cello	$12.99

Popular Hits
Breakeven • Fireflies • Halo • Hey, Soul Sister • I Gotta Feeling • I'm Yours • Need You Now • Poker Face • Viva La Vida • You Belong with Me • and more.

____	00842511	Flute	$12.99
____	00842512	Clarinet	$12.99
____	00842513	Alto Sax	$12.99
____	00842514	Tenor Sax	$12.99
____	00842515	Trumpet	$12.99
____	00842516	Horn	$12.99
____	00842517	Trombone	$12.99
____	00842518	Violin	$12.99
____	00842519	Viola	$12.99
____	00842520	Cello	$12.99

Songs from Frozen, Tangled and Enchanted
Do You Want to Build a Snowman? • For the First Time in Forever • Happy Working Song • I See the Light • In Summer • Let It Go • Mother Knows Best • That's How You Know • True Love's First Kiss • When Will My Life Begin • and more.

____	00126921	Flute	$12.99
____	00126922	Clarinet	$12.99
____	00126923	Alto Sax	$12.99
____	00126924	Tenor Sax	$12.99
____	00126925	Trumpet	$12.99
____	00126926	Horn	$12.99
____	00126927	Trombone	$12.99
____	00126928	Violin	$12.99
____	00126929	Viola	$12.99
____	00126930	Cello	$12.99

Women of Pop
Bad Romance • Jar of Hearts • Mean • My Life Would Suck Without You • Our Song • Rolling in the Deep • Single Ladies (Put a Ring on It) • Teenage Dream • and more.

____	00842650	Flute	$12.99
____	00842651	Clarinet	$12.99
____	00842652	Alto Sax	$12.99
____	00842653	Tenor Sax	$12.99
____	00842654	Trumpet	$12.99
____	00842655	Horn	$12.99
____	00842656	Trombone	$12.99
____	00842657	Violin	$12.99
____	00842658	Viola	$12.99
____	00842659	Cello	$12.99

Wicked
As Long As You're Mine • Dancing Through Life • Defying Gravity • For Good • I'm Not That Girl • Popular • The Wizard and I • and more.

____	00842236	Flute	$11.95
____	00842237	Clarinet	$11.99
____	00842238	Alto Saxophone	$11.95
____	00842239	Tenor Saxophone	$11.95
____	00842240	Trumpet	$11.99
____	00842241	Horn	$11.95
____	00842242	Trombone	$11.95
____	00842243	Violin	$11.99
____	00842244	Viola	$11.95
____	00842245	Cello	$11.99

FOR MORE INFORMATION, SEE YOUR LOCAL MUSIC DEALER, OR WRITE TO:

HAL·LEONARD® CORPORATION
7777 W. BLUEMOUND RD. P.O. BOX 13819 MILWAUKEE, WI 53213

0616

101 SONGS

YOUR FAVORITE SONGS ARE ARRANGED JUST FOR SOLO INSTRUMENTALISTS WITH THIS GREAT SERIES.

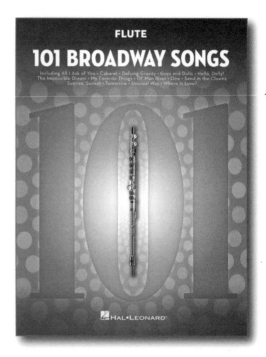

FLUTE
101 BROADWAY SONGS

Including All I Ask of You • Cabaret • Defying Gravity • Guys and Dolls • Hello, Dolly! • The Impossible Dream • My Favorite Things • Ol' Man River • One • Send in the Clowns • Sunrise, Sunset • Tomorrow • Unusual Way • Where Is Love?

VIOLIN
101 CLASSICAL THEMES

Including All the Things You Are • Bewitched • Fly Me to the Moon • How Deep Is the Ocean • I've Got the World on a String • In a Sentimental Mood • A Night in Tunisia • Stormy Weather • Unforgettable • Witchcraft

TRUMPET
101 JAZZ SONGS

Including All the Things You Are • Bewitched • Fly Me to the Moon • How Deep Is the Ocean • I've Got the World on a String • In a Sentimental Mood • A Night in Tunisia • Stormy Weather • Unforgettable • Witchcraft

101 BROADWAY SONGS

Any Dream Will Do • Cabaret • Defying Gravity • Do You Hear the People Sing? • Edelweiss • Getting to Know You • Guys and Dolls • Hello, Dolly! • I Dreamed a Dream • If I Were a Bell • Luck Be a Lady • Mame • The Music of the Night • Ol' Man River • People Will Say We're in Love • Seasons of Love • Send in the Clowns • The Surrey with the Fringe on Top • Think of Me • Tomorrow • What I Did for Love • You'll Never Walk Alone • and many more.

00154199	Flute	$14.99
00154200	Clarinet	$14.99
00154201	Alto Sax	$14.99
00154202	Tenor Sax	$14.99
00154203	Trumpet	$14.99
00154204	Horn	$14.99
00154205	Trombone	$14.99
00154206	Violin	$14.99
00154207	Viola	$14.99
00154208	Cello	$14.99

101 CLASSICAL THEMES

Ave Maria • Bist du bei mir (You Are with Me) • Canon in D • Clair de Lune • Dance of the Sugar Plum Fairy • 1812 Overture • Eine Kleine Nachtmusik ("Serenade"), First Movement Excerpt • The Flight of the Bumble Bee • Funeral March of a Marionette • Fur Elise • Gymnopedie No. 1 • Jesu, Joy of Man's Desiring • Lullaby • Minuet in G • Ode to Joy • Piano Sonata in C • Pie Jesu • Rondeau • Theme from Swan Lake • Wedding March • William Tell Overture • and many more.

00155315	Flute	$14.99
00155317	Clarinet	$14.99
00155318	Alto Sax	$14.99
00155319	Tenor Sax	$14.99
00155320	Trumpet	$14.99
00155321	Horn	$14.99
00155322	Trombone	$14.99
00155323	Violin	$14.99
00155324	Viola	$14.99
00155325	Cello	$14.99

101 JAZZ SONGS

All of Me • Autumn Leaves • Bewitched • Blue Skies • Body and Soul • Cheek to Cheek • Come Rain or Come Shine • Don't Get Around Much Anymore • A Fine Romance • Here's to Life • I Could Write a Book • It Could Happen to You • The Lady Is a Tramp • Like Someone in Love • Lullaby of Birdland • The Nearness of You • On Green Dolphin Street • Satin Doll • Stella by Starlight • Tangerine • Unforgettable • The Way You Look Tonight • Yesterdays • and many more.

00146363	Flute	$14.99
00146364	Clarinet	$14.99
00146366	Alto Sax	$14.99
00146367	Tenor Sax	$14.99
00146368	Trumpet	$14.99
00146369	Horn	$14.99
00146370	Trombone	$14.99
00146371	Violin	$14.99
00146372	Viola	$14.99
00146373	Cello	$14.99

HAL•LEONARD® CORPORATION
7777 W. BLUEMOUND RD. P.O. BOX 13819 MILWAUKEE, WI 53213

Prices, contents and availability subject to change without notice.